The Missions: California's Heritage

MISSION

SAN LUIS REY de FRANCIA

D0465562

by

Mary Null Boulé

Merryant Publishers, Inc.
10920 Palisades Ave. S.W.
Vashon, WA 98070
206-463-3879
Fax 206-463-1604
http://www.merryantpublishers.com

Book Eighteen in a series of twenty-one

With special thanks to Msgr. Francis J. Weber, Archivist of the Los Angeles Catholic Diocese for his encouragement and expertise in developing this series.

This series is dedicated to my sister, Nancy Null Kenyon, whose editing skills and support were so freely given.

Library of Congress Catalog Card Number: 89-90967

ISBN: 978-1-877599-17-0

Father Junípero Serra

INTRODUCTION

Building of a mission church involved everyone in the mission community. Priests were engineers and architects; Native Americans did the construction. Mission Indian in front is pouring adobe mix into a brick form. Bricks were then dried in the sun.

FATHER SERRA AND THE MISSIONS: AN INTRODUCTION

The year was 1769. On the east coast of what would soon become the United States, the thirteen original colonies were making ready to break away from England. On the west coast of our continent, however, there could be found only untamed land inhabited by Native Americans, or Indians. Although European explorers had sailed up and down the coast in their ships, no one but American Indians had explored the length of this land on foot . . . until now.

To this wild, beautiful country came a group of adventurous men from New Spain, as Mexico was then called. They were following the orders of their king, King Charles III of Spain.

One of the men was a Spanish missionary named Fray Junípero Serra. He had been given a tremendous job; especially since he was fifty-six years old, an old man in those days. King Charles III had ordered mission settlements to be built along the coast of Alta (Upper) California and it was Fr. Serra's task to carry out the king's wishes.

Father Serra had been born in the tiny village of Petra

on the island of Mallorca, Spain. He had done such an excellent job of teaching and working with the Indians in Mexican missions, the governor of New Spain had suggested to the king that Fr. Serra do the same with the Indians of Alta California. Hard-working Fray Serra was helped by Don Gaspár de Portolá, newly chosen governor of Alta California, and two other Franciscan priests who had grown up with Fr. Serra in Mallorca, Father Fermin Lasuén and Father Francisco Palóu.

There were several reasons why men had been told to build settlements along the coast of this unexplored country. First, missions would help keep the land as Spanish territory. Spain wanted to be sure the rest of the world knew it owned this rich land. Second, missions were to be built near harbors so towns would grow there. Ships from other countries could then stop to trade with the Spaniards, but these travelers could not try to claim the land for themselves. Third, missions were a good way to turn Indians into Christian, hard-working people.

It would be nice if we could write here that everything went well; that twenty-one missions immediately sprang up along the coast. Unfortunately, all did not go well. It would take fifty-four years to build all the California missions. During those fifty-four years many people died from Indian attacks, sickness, and starvation. Earthquakes and fires constantly ruined mission buildings, which then had to be built all over again. Fr. Serra calmly overcame each problem as it happened, as did those priests who followed him.

When a weary Fray Serra finally died in 1784, he had founded nine missions from San Diego to Monterey and had arranged the building of many more. Fr. Lasuén continued Fr. Serra's work, adding eight more missions to the California mission chain. The remaining four missions were founded in later years.

Originally, plans had been to place missions a hard day's walk from each other. Many of them were really quite far apart. Travelers truly struggled to go from one mission to another along the 650 miles of walking road known as El Camino Real, The Royal Highway. Today keen eyes will sometimes see tall, curved poles with bells hanging from them sitting by the side of streets and highways. These bell poles are marking a part of the old El Camino Real.

At first Spanish soldiers were put in charge of the towns which grew up near each mission. The priests were told to handle only the mission and its properties. It did not take long to realize the soldiers were not kind and gentle leaders. Many were uneducated and did not have the understanding they should have had in dealing with people. So the padres came to be in charge of not only the mission, but of the townspeople and even of the soldiers.

The first missions at San Diego and Monterey were built near the ocean where ships could bring them needed supplies. After early missions began to grow their own food and care for themselves, later mission compounds were built farther away from the coast. What one mission did well, such as leatherworking, candlemaking, or raising cattle, was shared with other missions. As a result, missions became somewhat specialized in certain products.

Although mission buildings looked different from mission to mission, most were built from one basic plan. Usually a compound was constructed as a large, four-sided building with an inner patio in the center. The outside of the quadrangle had only one or two doors, which were locked at night to protect the mission. A church usually sat at one corner of the quadrangle and was always the tallest and largest part of the mission compound.

Facing the inner patio were rooms for the two priests living there, workshops, a kitchen, storage rooms for grain and food, and the mission office. Rooms along the back of the quadrangle often served as home to the unmarried Indian women who worked in the kitchen. The rest of the Indians lived just outside the walls of the mission in their own village.

Beyond the mission wall and next to the church was a cemetery. Today you can still see many of the original headstones of those who died while living and working at the mission. Also outside the walls were larger workshops, a reservoir holding water used at the mission, and orchards containing fruit trees. Huge fields surrounded each mission where crops grew and livestock such as sheep, cattle, and horses grazed.

It took a great deal of time for some Indian tribes to under-stand the new way of life a mission offered, even though the

Native Americans always had food and shelter when they became mission Indians. Each morning all Indians were awakened at sunrise by a church bell calling them to church. Breakfast followed church . . . and then work. The women spun thread and made clothes, as well as cooked meals. Men and older boys worked in workshops or fields and constructed buildings. Meanwhile the Indian children went to school, where the padres taught them. After a noon meal there was a two hour rest before work began again. After dinner the Indians sang, played, or danced. This way of life was an enormous change from the less organized Indian life before the missionaries arrived. Many tribes accepted the change, some had more trouble getting used to a regular schedule, some tribes never became a part of mission life.

Water was all-important to the missions. It was needed to irrigate crops and to provide for the mission people and animals. Priests designed and engineered magnificent irrigation systems at most of the missions. All building of aqueducts and reservoirs of these systems was done by the mission Indians.

With all the organized hard work, the missions did very well. They grew and became strong. Excellent vineyards gave wine for the priests to use and to sell. Mission fields produced large grain crops of wheat and corn, and vast grazing land developed huge herds of cattle and sheep. Mission life was successful for over fifty years.

When Mexico broke away from Spain, it found it did not have enough money to support the California missions, as Spain had been doing. So in 1834, Mexico enforced the secularization law which their government had decreed several years earlier. This law stated missions were to be taken away from the missionaries and given to the Indians. The law said that if an Indian did not want the land or buildings, the property was to be sold to anyone who wished to buy it.

It is true the missions had become quite large and powerful. And as shocked as the padres were to learn of the secularization law, they also knew the missions had originally been planned as temporary, or short term projects. The priests had been sure their Indians would be well-trained enough to run the missions by themselves when the time came to move to other unsettled lands. In fact, however, even after fifty years the California Indians were still not ready to handle the huge missions.

Since the Indians did not wish to continue the missions, the buildings and land were sold, the Indians not even waiting for money or, in some cases, receiving money for the sale.

Sad times lay ahead. Many Indians went back to the old way of life. Some Indians stayed on as servants to the new owners and often these owners were not good to them. Mission buildings were used for everything from stores and saloons to animal barns. In one mission the church became a barracks for the army. A balcony was built for soldiers with their horses stabled in the altar area. Rats ate the stored grain and beautiful church robes. Furniture and objects left by the padres were stolen. People even stole the mission building roof tiles, which then caused the adobe brick walls to melt from rain. Earthquakes finished off many buildings.

Shortly after California became a part of the United States in the mid-1850s, our government returned all mission buildings to the Catholic Church. By this time most of them were in terrible condition. Since the priests needed only the church itself and a few rooms to live in, the other rooms of the mission were rented to anyone who needed them. Strange uses were found in some cases. In the San Fernando Mission, for example, there was once a pig farm in the patio area.

Tourists finally began to notice the mission ruins in the early 1900s. Groups of interested people got together to see if the missions could be restored. Some missions had been "modernized" by this time, unfortunately, but within the last thirty years historians have found enough pictures, drawings, and written descriptions to rebuild or restore most of the missions to their original appearances.

The restoration of all twenty-one missions is a splendid way to preserve our California heritage. It is the hope of many Californians that this dream of restoration can become a reality in the near future.

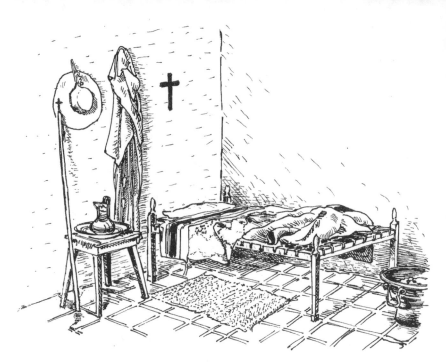

Recreation of a priest's bedroom is found in mission's excellent museum. Notice priest's hat and walking stick with cross atop it. These are only remaining ones from mission times.

Pepper tree known as the oldest in California, found in large cloistered patio behind convento.

MISSION SAN LUIS REY

I. THE MISSION TODAY

San Luis Rey has been called "King of the Missions" through the years for good reason. The mission sits grandly on a low hill five miles east of the city of Oceanside. It overlooks a growing valley in the town of San Luis Rey. Most of the quadrangle of the mission has been restored, although it is smaller in size than the original. Visitors may freely visit most of the mission. But a large patio in the back of the quadrangle is used only for people attending private religious meetings which the priests sponsor all year long. Inside this back patio stands what is thought to be the oldest pepper tree in California. The giant old tree is nearly two hundred years old.

At one time the trim of the church facade and cloister balcony was painted gold, but within the last few years the mission was repainted white and the gold trim has not been added. The buildings do not need gold trim to make them look majestic.

Twelve of the original thirty-two arches form the front corridor of the two-story cloister to the left of the church. The roof of the corridor forms a balcony to the rooms on the second story. A gift shop, offices, and a large museum fill the lower floor. The museum is one of the best of the California missions. It not only contains objects from Mission San Luis Rey's early days, but also church items from the much older Mexican missions. The only remaining original monk's, or friar's, hat and walking staff are found here. Re-creations of a mission kitchen, padre's bedroom-cell, workshop, and sacristy have been set up to show mission life. Of special interest is a copper baptismal font brought by Father Junipero Serra to Mission San Diego, the first mission. There is also a chest of drawers for holding priest robes that was used by Fr. Serra and brought from Spain on the first ship to Upper California in 1769. In one corner is a large, very old, music choir book with pages made of sheepskin. One charming item is a creche handcarved by an Indian during mission days.

11

Behind the museum is an inner garden area surrounded by an inner quadrangle of two-story adobe where the present priests and brothers live. At one time the missison was a seminary where young men studied to be priests. Today, however, the priests who live here act as parish priests in addition to conducting private retreats.

To the right of the front cloister is the beautifully restored church. Its facade has fake pillars, or pilasters, on either side of the double door entrance. At the top, the facade has been shaped with curved and curled edges to form a tall triangle-shaped wall above the roof line. Three niches on the lower part of the facade hold statues. There is a deep round window above the arched entrance to the church. To the right of the facade is a large, but graceful, domed bell tower. The church walls vary in thickness from six to nine feet. A white adobe wall encloses the old cemetery to the right of the church.

The inside of the church measures 180 feet long, 28 feet wide, and 30 feet high. This makes it one of the larger mission churches. It is richly decorated in restored Indian fresco designs painted to match pictures of the original designs. The warm colors of rust and blue make the church seem to welcome those who enter. To the left, just inside the entrance, is the baptistry with its domed ceiling and painted pillars. The original Indian-made adobe and brick pedestal in the center holds the original copper baptismal font.

One of the most beautiful rooms in any of the missions opens off the right wall opposite the baptistry. Named the Madonna Chapel, it was the mortuary chapel in mission days where bodies were prepared for burial. It is a large round room with a high domed ceiling. The walls are brightly decorated in Indian designs. Many old paintings hang on the wall. A lovely statue of the Madonna stands above the recessed altar where the bodies were laid. Two tunnels, one on each side of the altar, have often been called mysterious. Actually, the tunnel on the left was for the padre to reach the altar when a body blocked his way. The tunnel on the right leads to a hidden balcony above the altar, where the loved ones could look down upon the body privately.

The Stations of the Cross on the walls of the main part, or proper, of the church were painted especially for San Luis Rey.

Artists in Mexico painted them sometime in the 1780s, before the mission had even been founded. One other painting on the wall dates back to Fr. Serra's time.

San Luis Rey's church is the only one other than San Juan Capistrano's ruined church which was built in the form of a cross. The "arms" of the cross are the side altars of the sanctuary. An altar rail stands in front of the side altars. Above the transept, where the cross-arms meet, is an exquisitely built eight-sided dome of narrow wood boards that rise to an eight-sided window tower at the top. This domed ceiling is the only one of its kind in the California Mission System.

The wood pulpit high on the left wall near the sanctuary is original, the only original wood object not ruined by termites through the years. The ceiling beams and floor tiles have all had to be replaced.

The original reredos was square-shaped and painted with gold paint. It was torn to pieces by treasure-seekers sometime during the forty-six years no priest lived at the mission, when a story was told about treasure being hidden within it. No attempt was made to rebuild the reredos as it had been, for no pictures or drawings of it have ever been found. The present reredos was built to match the decorations of the side altars. At the top stands the satue of Saint Louis IX, King of France, patron saint of the mission. A large crucifix hangs just above the altar.

Mission San Luis Rey still has in its possession the original document signed by Abraham Lincoln, restoring the mission property to church ownership. Of this the mission people are rightfully proud. But San Luis Rey Mission also has the same warm feeling of hospitality about it that its own Father Peyri shared with the visitors of long ago. Now, that is something about which the mission today can really be proud.

II. HISTORY OF THE MISSION

The eighteenth mission of the California missions, Mission San Luis Rey de Francia, was founded by Father Fermin Lasuén on June 13, 1798. Named for Saint Louis IX, King of France in the 1200s, it was the last mission founded by Fr. Lasuén, who was over seventy years old at the time. Fr. Lasuén did not choose this site so much for the good soil. In fact, he felt the soil might not be as rich as some of the other mission sites.

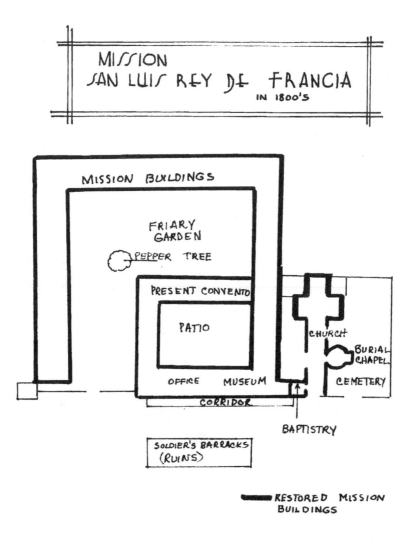

MISSION
SAN LUIS REY DE FRANCIA
IN 1800'S

MISSION BUILDINGS

FRIARY GARDEN

PEPPER TREE

PRESENT CONVENTO

PATIO

CHURCH

BURIAL CHAPEL

OFFICE   MUSEUM

CEMETERY

CORRIDOR

BAPTISTRY

SOLDIER'S BARRACKS
(RUINS)

RESTORED MISSION BUILDINGS

He decided this was a good place for a mission because of the great numbers of Native Americans living in the area. He liked how good-natured these Indians were.

It was an excellent choice, as Father Anthony Peyri who was put in charge of the new mission soon found out. What is more, even the soil turned out to be very good. The mission was a success from the start. The natives loved to work hard and were willing to be baptized in the church. Within three weeks the Indians had made 6,000 adobe bricks to begin mission buildings.

The first church of adobe brick was large enough to hold 1,000 Indians. It was completed in 1820 and had a tile roof. By 1804 the inner patio had been enclosed. There was tile-roofed housing for priests, soldiers, and the young native women. Although it was only six years since the founding of the mission, crops already averaged 5,000 bushels a year and there were over 10,000 large animals in the mission herds.

Father Peyri's amazing talent for designing and building really began to show in 1811 when work was started on the magnificent church we see today, restored. The church was dedicated four years later, in 1815, but it was enlarged and improved for nearly ten more years after the dedication. A French visitor in 1826 described the mission as looking like "a palace."

While the good padre, Fr. Peyri, was building his huge mission, he was also in charge of training Indians to produce butter, tallow for candles and soap, leather products, wine, oil, woven cloth, and how to cook. He also showed the mission Indians how to grow such crops as corn, wheat, and beans. Indians became cowboys who could handle the cattle and horses. Many of them were taught to sing harmony in the church choir. Most of the natives loved music. Because mission priests could not take care of all of these responsibilities alone, padres such as Fr. Peyri chose Indian leaders called alcaldes to help the soldiers take charge of the workers. One of the alcaldes' jobs was to spread the news of what the priest needed done each day. A priest, with a few alcaldes and soldiers, could keep hundreds of Native Americans busy and productive this way.

By 1826, the San Luis Rey quadrangle measured 500 feet along each side. The front of the quadrangle was called the cloister and had rooms for the priests and for visiting guests. There was an infirmary where the priests took care of the sick, as well as living quarters for women, storerooms, and workrooms all within the quadrangle. Huge orchards and gardens were located right outside the mission walls.

Perhaps the most interesting of all at San Luis Rey was a tremendous lavanderia, or laundry, built at the bottom of the steep hill in front of the mission. This area became known as the sunken gardens because of the exotic plants growing there. Water flowed naturally from two springs through the carved mouths of stone gargoyles into bricked areas so the Indian women could wash clothes. A charcoal filter was put there to purify the water for drinking after it had been used. It is awesome to view the fifty-some side brick steps leading down to the lavanderia.

In the early 1830s the mission was enjoying its most prosperous time, with 2,800 natives living at the mission. It was at this best of times that the Mexican government, which had broken away from Spain's rule, took over the management of the California missions. Fr. Peyri tried very hard to get along with the Mexican officials and for a while the mission at San Luis Rey continued to grow. But the poor Spanish padre finally realized that after thiry-three years he must leave his beloved mission and Indians. One night in 1832, he secretly left, hoping to keep from making sad goodbyes to his Indians. He was immediately missed the next morning and a large group of mission Indians rushed to the San Diego harbor just in time to see his ship sailing for Mexico. The Indians prayed for his return for many years after that, but he never came back.

Secularization laws were put into force by Mexico two years after Fr. Peyri left. According to these laws, land was supposed to be given back to the Indians. But greedy Mexican officials bought or sold mission lands, keeping the money for themselves. One of the worst officials was the then governor of California, Pio Pico, who finally sold what was left of Mission San Luis Rey's buildings for $2,437. The true value of the land at the time was over $200,000.

Even though the United States returned the mission buildings to the Catholic Church in 1861, no religious services were held there for 46 years. In 1892, two Mexican padres asked for and got permission to restore the mission as a monastery for refugee Mexican Franciscan monks. Father Joseph J. O'Keefe, an American Franciscan priest, was assigned to the mission to act as an interpreter for the Spanish-speaking monks. In 1895, he was promoted to superior of the mission and began to rebuild the old ruins.

Fr. O'Keefe's first years were spent building temporary quarters for the twenty-five Mexican priests and brothers, and repairing the church. By 1903, the second part of restoration was started: that of rebuilding the quadrangle as a permanent living quarters for the thirteen remaining refugees still living there. The new quadrangle was restored enough for them to move in by 1905.

It was just as the living quarters were completed when the Mexican order of priests stopped sending people to the mission. This left Fr. O'Keefe without money to continue his restoration, so in 1912 he managed to convince his own Franciscan order to accept care of the mission and its rebuilding project. By this time, however, he was a tired old man. After spending nineteen years of his life restoring San Luis Rey, Fr. O'Keefe asked to be retired to Santa Bárbara. His request was granted and he died there three years later.

Throughout the years since his death, the mission restoration has continued. In 1926, a corner of the bell tower collapsed and was repaired. In 1951, the mission was rededicated after major restoration of two wings of the quadrangle. In 1959, the lavanderia and sunken garden were uncovered from layers of dirt that had slowly covered the area through the years.

Today Mission San Luis Rey is a working mission, kept in excellent condition by a parish of caring people. It glows as it did over 150 years ago when Fr. Peyri lovingly tended his magnificent "palace."

Dignified reredos in sanctuary is not like original, since no pictures of original were ever found. In ceiling in front of sanctuary lower part of the unique wooden dome, topped by large glass-paned lantern can be seen.

Lovely, domed Madonna Chapel was once mission's burial preparation room. Tunnel on right leads to balcony overlooking altar so mourners could view the body in private. Tunnel to left took priest behind altar for burial services.

OUTLINE OF
MISSION SAN LUIS REY

I. **The mission today**
   A. Title given to mission
   B. Location
   C. Mission quadrangle
      1. Smaller size today
      2. Trim on facade and old cloister
      3. Arches
         a. Number yesterday and today
      4. Gift shop and offices
   D. Museum
      1. Religious objects from San Luis Rey and Mexican missions
         a. Friar's hat and walking stick
         b. Chest of drawers for priest's robes
         c. Copper font from San Diego
         d. Music choir book
      2. Re-creations
         a. Sacristy
         b. Kitchen
         c. Workshop
         d. Padre's bedroom-cell
   E. Inner quadrangle and garden patio
   F. Church exterior
      1. Description of facade
      2. Bell tower
      3. Cemetery and adobe wall
   G. Church interior
      1. Size
      2. Decoration of walls
      3. Baptistry
         a. Font
      4. Madonna Chapel
      5. Stations of the Cross
      6. Shape of church
         a. Sanctuary with side altars
         b. Dome with eight sides
      7. Wood pulpit
      8. Reredos
         a. Style
         b. Patron saint statue

Outline continued next page

II. History of the mission

A. Founding
   1. Fr. Lasuén
   2. Date
   3. Site and why chosen
B. Father Anthony Peyri
   1. His early days at mission
      a. First adobe church description
      b. First quadrangle buildings
      c. Fr. Peyri's ability to design buildings
   2. Mission in 1804
C. Present day church
   1. Date begun
   2. Date dedicated
   3. Improving the church
D. Mission life
   1. Training of the Indians
   2. Alcaldes and soldiers
E. Mission in 1826
   1. Quadrangle buildings
F. Lavanderia
   1. Location
   2. Description
G. 1830
   1. Mexican management of mission
   2. Fr. Peyri's leaving
H. Secularization
   1. Mexican officials' stealing of the land
   2. San Luis Rey sold
      a. Price
I. Church without priests - 1846-1892
J. 1892
   1. Seminary begun for refugees from Mexico
   2. Fr. O'Keefe arrives
K. Restoration
   1. First years with Fr. O'Keefe
   2. Second part of restoration
   3. Refugee priests leave
   4. American Francescans continue restoration
   5. Father O'Keefe retires
   6. Bell tower
   7. Rededication 1951
   8. Lavanderia uncovered in 1959

GLOSSARY

BUTTRESS:	a large mass of stone or wood used to strengthen buildings
CAMPANARIO:	a wall which holds bells
CLOISTER:	an enclosed area; a word often used instead of convento
CONVENTO:	mission building where priests lived
CORRIDOR:	covered, outside hallway found at most missions
EL CAMINO REAL:	highway between missions; also known as The King's Highway
FACADE:	front wall of a building
FONT:	large, often decorated bowl containing Holy Water for baptizing people
FOUNDATION:	base of a building, part of which is below the ground
FRESCO:	designs painted directly on walls or ceilings
LEGEND:	a story coming from the past
PORTICO:	porch or covered outside hallway
PRESERVE:	to keep in good condition without change
PRESIDIO:	a settlement of military men
QUADRANGLE:	four-sided shape; the shape of most missions

RANCHOS: large ranches often many miles from mission proper where crops were grown and animal herds grazed

REBUILD: to build again; to repair a great deal of something

REPLICA: a close copy of the original

REREDOS: the wall behind the main altar inside the church

*RESTORATION: to bring something back to its original condition (see * below)

SANCTUARY: area inside, at the front of the church where the main altar is found

SECULARIZATION: something not religious; a law in mission days taking the mission buildings away from the church and placing them under government rule

*ORIGINAL: the first one; the first one built

BIBLIOGRAPHY

Bauer, Helen. *California Mission Days*. Sacramento, CA: California Department of Education, 1957.

Bonestell, Chesley and Paul Johnson. *The Golden Era of the Missions*. San Francisco, CA 94102: Chronicle Books, 1974.

Goodman, Marian. *Missions of California*. Redwood City, CA: Redwood City Tribune, 1962.

Sunset Editors. *The California Missions*. Menlo Park, CA: Lane Publishing Company, 1979.

Weber, Francis J. *King of the Missions*. Hong Kong: Libra Press Limited, no date.

Wright, Ralph B., ed. *California Missions*. Arroyo Grande, CA 93420: Hubert A. Lowman, 1977.

Pamphlet. *Mission San Luis Rey* Old Mission, San Luis Rey, CA 92068: Franciscan Padres, no date.

For more information about this mission, write to:

Mission San Luis Rey
4050 Mission Avenue
San Luis Rey, CA 92068

It is best to enclose a self-addressed, stamped envelope and a small amount of money to pay for brochures and pictures the mission might send you.

CREDITS

Cover art and Father Serra Illustration: Ellen Grim
Illustrations: Alfredo de Batuc
Ground Layout: Mary Boule'
Printing: Print NW, Tacoma, Washington